# Touched
# By
# A
# Thought

*Brian G. O'Rourke*

*A Writer's Artistry*
*Words about Life, God, You and Me.*

SUNSTONE
PRESS

Illustrations by William Shedd

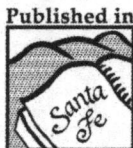

Sunstone books may be purchased for educational, business, or sales promo-
tional use.
For information please write: Special Markets Department, Sunstone Press,
P.O. Box 2321, Santa Fe, New Mexico 87504-2321.

Library of Congress Cataloging-in-Publication Data:

O'Rourke, Brian G., 1952–
    Touched by a thought: a writer's artistry, words about life,
God, you and me / Brian G. O'Rourke.
        p. cm.
    ISBN: 0-86534-335-7
        1. Meditations. I. Title.

BL624.2 .O67  2002
291.4'32—dc21                                                    2002022766

Published in SUNSTONE PRESS
            Post Office Box 2321
            Santa Fe, NM 87504-2321 / USA
            (505) 988-4418 / *orders only* (800) 243-5644
            FAX (505) 988-1025
            **www.sunstonepress.com**

**This book is dedicated to the love of four incredible women who have blessed my life.**

**My Mother, Isobel**
Like many children, I believe my Mother is God's greatest gift. My Mom is wrapped in a small human frame filled with goodness, generosity and sensitivity. I have an endless smile when I think of this special lady, who has been the fountain of my life.

**Sandy**
The mother of our three children, Sandy is a special spirit, a gift given to others so that we may know that the uniqueness of life is to be shared selflessly.

**Jennifer**
My beautiful daughter who has blest my life with more smiles, more love, and more warmth than I ever knew possible. The appreciation I have to God for the gift of my daughter is beyond expression.

**Krista**
The angel guided by God to show me the peaceful, loving appreciation for life. A spirituality and inward beauty, Krista epitomizes the natural way to live life in God's love—throughout eternity.

God Bless Each of You
Much Thanks
I Love You!

**This book is dedicated to the love of four incredible women who have blessed my life.**

**My Mother, Isobel**
Like many children, I believe my Mother is God's greatest gift. My Mom is wrapped in a small human frame filled with goodness, generosity and sensitivity. I have an endless smile when I think of this special lady, who has been the fountain of my life.

**Sandy**
The mother of our three children, Sandy is a special spirit, a gift given to others so that we may know that the uniqueness of life is to be shared selflessly.

**Jennifer**
My beautiful daughter who has blest my life with more smiles, more love, and more warmth than I ever knew possible. The appreciation I have to God for the gift of my daughter is beyond expression.

**Krista**
The angel guided by God to show me the peaceful, loving appreciation for life. A spirituality and inward beauty, Krista epitomizes the natural way to live life in God's love—throughout eternity.

God Bless Each of You
Much Thanks
I Love You!

## Life is a spiritual journey, the exploration of Oneness

In this book, *Touched By A Thought,* I hope you will sense the experience of an ordinary life through which we all pass to be with the God of creation, the God of Love.

The feelings of peacefulness, the struggle of society's structure, the joy of togetherness, the pain of prejudice and the love of life's uniqueness, perhaps will be found in your thoughts and interpretation of these written works.

Words are so precious. May the words in these written works touch your thoughts about life, God, you and me.

God Bless
Brian G. O'Rourke

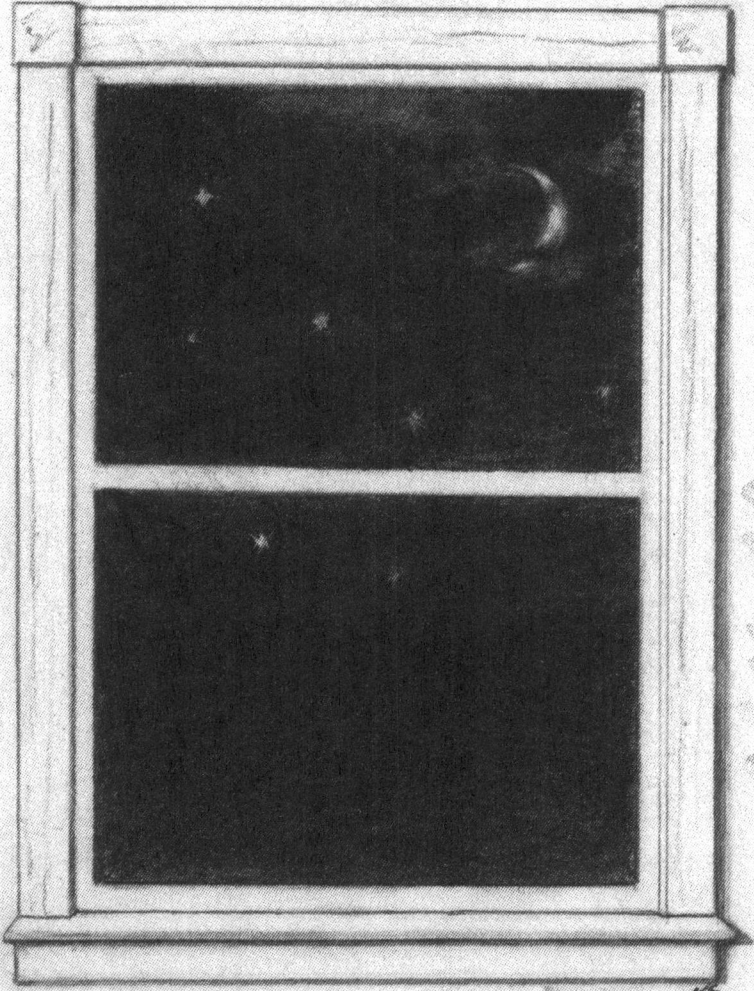

Our thought is God's creativity.
Our creativity is God's thought.

## God's Next Child

Through the window shines a light
To a peaceful place seldom seen.
A solemn friend with crying eyes
Is quietly here, accepting us in all of life.

In the window there is a telling sign
Of love's only chance.
In a moment of devotion,
Is the birth and beauty
Of God's next child.

## Tomorrow's Path

I can not start over
I can only
continue the journey forward
towards tomorrow's path
of acceptance,
love and oneness
with God, you and me.

## It's Never Too Late

It's Never Too Late
To read a book to a child,
To smile at a lost friend,
To forgive,
To care about everyone,
To hold someone's hand,
To pray,
To try again,
To befriend an enemy,
To have fun,
To learn something new,
To hug someone special,
To say, I love you.

I love you.

## One Friend

If the silence of the heart is revealed
In the moments that life gives us,
Our soul will be filled with feelings
So that one friend may love another.

Be a gift to every life you touch
And graciously accept the gifts
Of those lives that touch you.

## Confirmation

Look deep into the eyes of a child
And there you will see
The love of each parent,
The love of God
And the confirmation of life's
Continuing spiritual journey.

## Life Is

Life is not what you have
Or don't have.
Life is not what you know
Or don't know.
Life is not where you get to go
Or don't get to go.
Life is not where you live
Or don't live.
Life is not who your friends are
Or who are not your friends.

Life is why God created you.
Life is that God created you.
Life is for giving thanks.
Life is for being blest.
Life is to discover
Who you are!

## Visions

Have visions beyond your horizons
To the bluest of skies, pale white clouds
and
Endless dreams.
Forever is there, somewhere beyond time
Where the whys are explained
And the sunlight of God's love
Is found within.

## Our Prayer

We pray and give thanks for,

you
me
us

our friends
all children
our families

the dog next door
snow

your dreams and our hopes

and God's love.

The magnificence of God's creation
is such,
That no-one may fully comprehend,
at least for now.

## I've Known

I've known your friendship,
      your passion,
      your heart,
      and I love you.

I've known our similarities,
      our differences,
      our struggles,
      and I love you.

I've known my dreams,
      your dreams,
      our dreams,
      and I love you.

I've known your love,
      my love for you,
      our love,
      and I thank God for this life.

## Come Talk With Me

Come talk with me
I asked God one day.
Listen to my plea.
Tell me how to be.
God, I need to know
Will you come talk with me?

God is listening, as I always do
Were the words heard inside of me.
You are doing just fine
And I am here to speak through you
For life and God are One in time.

## Only In

Only in the giving of yourself,
Only in appreciation,
Only in the peace of all people,
Only in silence,
Only in the friendship of others,
Only in selflessness,
Only in the family of mankind,
Only in acceptance,
Only in the prayer of openness,
Only in wholesomeness,
Only in the pain of struggling,
Only in remembering,
Only in the Oneness of creation,
Only in love
Is the spirit found experiencing God.

In this life
I have loved no one more than you.

## The Love That I Am

Love is the essence of God.
When I am able to express love
I am able to feel it.
When I am able to feel love
I am able to know it.
When I am able to know love
I am able to fully embrace it.
When I am able to fully embrace love
I am able to be love.
The love that I am, I offer to you.

## Not Yet

Witness the remnants of my life
In finding the memories now forgotten
Of a love lost in this human time.

Gaze into my eyes,
Notice an empty heart.
Search my spirit,
Encounter a saddened soul.
Hold me so you may know a wholeness,
Not yet realized,
Not yet shared,
Not yet complete.

## Something To Say

When we were kids
We had something to say.
We did not know.
We did not know it all.
We were kids with something to say.
In looking back on all of it today
The learning was free
If we wanted it to be
Or the learning was tough.
More often than not the learning was rough.
Now in sharing the knowledge of life
With the next grown-ups to be
We are told everything will be okay
For they're just kids with something to say.

## May The God

May the God
Who nourishes your journey,
Who brings you love,
Who comforts your pain,
Who offers you new experiences,
Who rejoices in your accomplishments,
Who prays with you always,
Who created your uniqueness,
Bless and guide you
And all those you love.

Write the words to your own song,
Make your own music,
And share the sounds of life
With someone special.

## My

This is my voice.
The voice of thought
Found in the silence of prayer,
Endlessly reaching to be heard.

This is my life.
The spirit of creation,
Experiencing the wonder of all
That is known and unknown.

This is my love
Surrendering to the simplicity
Of acceptance
In all that is you,
In all that is God.

## In This Life I Pray

In this life I pray
I will be able to embrace
your love,
your tenderness,
your uniqueness,
your spirituality,
and our oneness.

## Think of Life

Think of life as a beautiful stream
Refreshingly clear and flowing free.
A peacefulness found in the quietness
Much like the forest in all of its green.
Think of life as it was meant to be,
Strolling harmoniously through given time,
Seeing beyond the horizon of blue,
A perfect picture of playfulness and beauty.
Think of a life experienced by you.

## You May Know

In a moment of silence
Hear the sounds of your soul.
Feel the love in your heart
So you may know
This is a life of eternity
With God, you and me.

The view of a morning horizon
Brings us closer to knowing
The beginning of light,
The end to darkness.

## urrender

.ook closely at the reflection
.n the mirror of life.
Observe the eyes of softness
without the tears.
Anticipate the warmth of a smile
upon the face of acceptance.
Be still in the palm of the hand of eternity.
Touch the gentle, peaceful heart
of Oneness with creation.
See yourself as you are seen from above
as you surrender to the secret
of this journey
Within the endless depths
of God's love.

## There Is...

At first, there were no words.
Then, slowly came those words.
At first, there was no love.
Then, slowly came the love.
I will account for the past,
I will account for the far,
I know this love will last
Beyond the light of the nearest star.
But, it is now when we should start
Our beginning.
For next, there is everything.
Last ... there is...

## Words

So many words have been written.
I too have shared a few,
Challenging the path of direction
Of what was meant to be.
In this generation not unlike all of life itself
I struggle, as I am sure you have too.
If only to know a reason
For all that is,
For all that was,
For all that will ever be
In God's journey of creating
You and me.

## I Love You, Mom

There was a moment in time
I first opened my eyes.
Although I do not remember my birth,
I knew you were the tender one,
The love that carried me to my life.
I love you, Mom.

In all that has changed
I still hold on to the memories
Filled with the sound of your voice,
The warmth of your smile,
The pride in your eyes,
The softness of your hugs
As you encouraged the dreams of life
Which made it so easy to express how much
I love you, Mom.

The remembrance of your kiss
That wiped away my tears,
The guidance of your touch
To keep me secure in a world of discovery,
Has taught me why
I love you, Mom.

Keeping the sun from setting
On these days now spent apart
Are the thoughts of the wonder you gave to life
And all the reasons through my tears
I am blest to say
I love you, Mom.

Love is the essence of life.
I love you
For being who you are.

## The Path

Remembering the yesterdays
In life's challenges not yet understood.
A childhood lost in its innocence
An adulthood found much too early.
Loved ones left in emptiness
As the journey falters on the path of fear.

If only life would accept
In the picture of God's plan
The creation of togetherness,
Then returning home is all but certain
And that is all we would ever ask.

## Ever Felt More Loved?

Have you ever felt more loved,
Perhaps, when standing in a room full of friends,
Singing songs and telling stories,
Watching daylight fade to return again?

Have you ever felt more loved,
Perhaps, when standing in a room full of friends,
A time when dreams are revealed,
And memories are made and shared?

Have you ever felt more loved,
Perhaps, when standing in a room full of friends,
Being a little mischievous,
Holding hands and finding a hug?

Have you ever felt more loved,
Perhaps, when standing in a room full of friends,
Laughing and crying,
And just being yourself?

Have you ever felt more loved,
Perhaps, when standing in a room full of friends?

**Your**

The birth of a thought through its expression
When spoken as the offspring of a feeling;
A moment of love shared
through words with a friend;
I am touched by Your hand
to be able to give again.

In Your words and in Your dreams for me,
I will remember where I found Your answer.

Just a short visit to feel Your presence,
I will be blessed with the willingness to care.

In each turn of sunshine to shade
Surrounded by beauty and held in Your love,
I am thankful for Your truth of tomorrow.

## A Golden Sunset

A golden sunset on canvas,
Silhouettes of who we were to be.
Earth-tone colors paint the way
Of promises framed and hung on the wall.
All was certain except for the how,
Yet it turned out to be a tempestuous time
In looking back some years from now.
The journeys not separate in the strife
Nor together in the fall of life
But joined forever in the spirit of it all.

We are,

One in God
One in Love
One in Spirit
One in Eternity

## An Angel

An angel stands before me
With an outreached hand, a helpful hug
And guidance known only by God.

The mysteries aren't mysteries anymore
As love has covered my life
In a peaceful blanket of acceptance.

There is not much left to be said
As my heart now speaks from my soul
Of the simple treasures of this life.

When you lay next to me
In a warmth found in eternity
The secrets of our love shared in Oneness
Will bring me back to the beginning of a journey
That has been blest for knowing you.

## Two Rings

Two rings reflecting the light,
The love of another,
Worn for life.
Two rings side by side together,
Sharing of souls in parallel lives.
Today, tomorrow, in time to mold forever.
Two rings simple in beauty,
Crafted in their likeness
And blest for Oneness.
Two rings,
Two hearts,
One life.

## Will Always Be

Empty in this experience of lost time
    Is the wonder of the inward choice
    To be as one is born
    Or to live as one is taught.

With all the beauty of our gifts
    Is the reflection of the fear.
    Are we truly part of the sacred truth,
    Or will we be vanished beyond
    The possibility of a chosen few.

I must tell you for I am sure
    God is not that way.
    With the thought of eternity
    Was the promise of life's first day,
    And all of God's creation,
    Will always be.

## Love

Through Love,
With Love,
In Love,
In unity with the Spirit,
All glory and honor is ours,
Forever and ever.

Peace is something we all want
yet we have not made peace important enough
to find.
Peace be with you
and
with all those you love.

## You Please

cean rain, spring-time trees,
fe-long friends and childhood dreams.
uiet mornings, mischievous schemes,
unning rivers and a summer night breeze.
ove filled hugs, forgotten memories,
layful days and autumn leaves.
ainbow skies, winter's first freeze,
A neighborhood party and baked Brie cheese.
All of God's creations, if you please.

## An Act of Love

At the bottom of my soul is a tear,
>left there as a reminder of a time
>when true friendship and love
>were found
>in the struggle and pain of life.

On my face is a smile,
>a peacefulness
>created by an act of love
>from God and you,
>to me.

## God Will Be With Us

Where is the entrance to and the boundaries of,
The place all of life aspires to obtain.
With no beginning and an end never seen,
Where is eternity, the heaven of my dream.
In just a blink of life's existence
A reward for the values and morals
The choices once made in haste,
Will be given so it is taught
To those of worthiness
But not to those of not.
It is in the structure of God's creation
That all the children will be blest,
So it is for you and it is for me
That God will be with us when we rest.

## God Will Have Seen It All

God will have seen it all,
The beginning to here and now
The choices that are chosen
The myths that justify our law.

God will have seen it all,
Our love held for ransom
Young lives kept subdued
An ancestor's path not right for you.

God will have seen it all,
Hatred, rage, misguided fear for naught
Our religious way is the only one
As so many faiths have taught.

God will have seen it all,
Loneliness a part of the day
Separation from the Creator
Forgiveness not offered in a loving way.

God will have seen it all,
Until that One lasting choice
A song of Oneness,
Sung with a single voice.

When you understand
The future of your journey
You will know how to love in living life.

## Be Still

Close the eyes
Quiet the mind
Open the heart
Soften the touch
Listen impartially
Inhale the breath of life
Be still
In the peacefulness of yourself
The Creator has been found.
Say hello.

## May

Within the humanness of life
May love be experienced,
May spirituality be understood,
May God be found everywhere,
May Oneness be known by all.

## There Is So Much

There is so much to witness beyond
The language, the gender,
The age, the experiences,
The color of skin, the social status.

There is so much to comprehend beyond
The level of education, the neighborhood,
The religious affiliation, the birth place of life,
The sexual preference, the political stances.

There is so much to embrace beyond
Someone's present journey
To the depth of each soul
And the love given by God,
To all, to everything.

There is so much to appreciate beyond
That which defines our uniqueness,
Our equality, our love, our Oneness,
In life, in creation, in eternity.

## I Pray For You

Thirty years is a life-time ago
When a dream was born
With a birth, the beginning of love.
Could it have not been known
So much would be lost
As time tempers the truth
And feelings are no longer free.
I pray for you.
Will you pray for me?

## Let Me Be

Let me be the will of God,
Let me be.
Let me be the voice of reason,
Let me be.
Let me be the heart of passion,
Let me be.
Let me be the path to peace,
Let me be.
Let me be the song of sincerity,
Let me be.
Let me be the reflection of choice,
Let me be.
Let me be the silent soul,
Let me be.
Let me be the creator of love,
Let me be.

Let me be me.